JUNIOR BIOS

Mindy Kaling

BY NORA GARDINER

Enslow PUBLISHING

Please visit our website, www.enslow.com. For a free color catalog of all our high-quality books, call toll free 1-800-398-2504 or fax 1-877-980-4454.

Library of Congress Cataloging-in-Publication Data

Names: Gardiner, Nora, author.
Title: Mindy Kaling / Nora Gardiner.
Description: New York : Enslow Publishing, [2022] | Series: Junior bios | Includes index.
Identifiers: LCCN 2020036879 (print) | LCCN 2020036880 (ebook) | ISBN 9781978525481 (library binding) | ISBN 9781978525467 (paperback) | ISBN 9781978525474 (set) | ISBN 9781978525498 (ebook)
Subjects: LCSH: Kaling, Mindy--Juvenile literature. | Actors--United States--Biography--Juvenile literature.
Classification: LCC PN2287.K18 G (print) | LCC PN2287.K18 (ebook) | DDC 791.4502/8092 [B]--dc23
LC record available at https://lccn.loc.gov/2020036879
LC ebook record available at https://lccn.loc.gov/2020036880

First Edition

Published in 2022 by
Enslow Publishing
29 E. 21st Street
New York, NY 10010

Designer: Deanna Paternostro
Editor: Kate Mikoley

Photo credits: Cover, p. 1 (Mindy Kaling) Amy Sussman/Staff/Getty Images Entertainment/Getty Images; cover, p. 1 (photo frame) Aleksandr Andrushkiv/Shutterstock.com; marble texture used throughout HardtIllustrations/Shutterstock.com; lined paper texture used throughout Mtsaride/Shutterstock.com; watercolor texture used throughout solarbird/Shutterstock.com; p. 5 Rich Fury/VF20/Contributor/Getty Images Entertainment/Getty Images; p. 7 Featureflash Photo Agency/Shutterstock.com; pp. 9, 13 Jeff Kravitz/Contributor/FilmMagic, Inc/Getty Images; p. 11 Frederick M. Brown/Stringer/Getty Images Entertainment/Getty Images; p. 14 Neilson Barnard/Staff/Getty Images Entertainment/Getty Images; p. 15 FOX/Contributor/FOX Image Collection/Getty Images; p. 17 Michael S. Schwartz/Contributor/FilmMagic/Getty Images; p. 19 Ian West - PA Images/Contributor/PA Images/Getty Images.

Printed in the United States of America

CPSIA compliance information: Batch #CWENS22: For further information contact Enslow Publishing, New York, New York, at 1-800-398-2504.

Contents

Words in the glossary appear in **bold** type the first time they are used in the text.

Her Own Boss

Mindy Kaling owes much of her success to one thing: She's created her own opportunities. Mindy has starred in her own TV show, created shows that feature **diverse** casts, and become a star as a writer, actress, and **producer**.

FACTS BEHIND THE FIGURE

Mindy's name at birth was Vera Mindy Chokalingam.

MINDY IS BEST KNOWN FOR WRITING AND ACTING IN COMEDIES, OR TV SHOWS AND MOVIES THAT ARE MEANT TO BE FUNNY.

Mindy was born on June 24, 1979. Her parents were Indian **immigrants** to the United States. Mindy's dad was an **architect** and her mom was a doctor. Mindy has an older brother named Vijay. They grew up in Cambridge, Massachusetts.

Young Writer

Mindy has always loved comedy! As a little girl, she wrote her own plays. When she was a teenager, she and her friends watched lots of comedy TV shows and movies. Soon, she was writing her own **sketches** and filming them!

FACTS BEHIND THE FIGURE

Writing on *Late Night with Conan O'Brien* was Mindy's dream job.

MINDY LEFT COLLEGE WITH AN IDEA OF HOW HER LIFE WOULD GO. SHE LATER SPOKE AT THE DARTMOUTH GRADUATION AND SAID: "DON'T BE SCARED IF YOU DON'T DO THINGS IN THE RIGHT ORDER, OR IF YOU DON'T DO SOME THINGS AT ALL."

Mindy went to Dartmouth College. She acted in and wrote plays while there. Mindy was an **intern** at *Late Night with Conan O'Brien* too. In July 2001, Mindy moved to New York City with some friends.

The Play's the Thing

Mindy tried out for a few jobs in New York, but nothing came of them. She worked as a babysitter and as a production assistant on a small TV show. She and her friend, Brenda Withers, wanted to be doing something more creative.

In Her Own Words

"If I can give one bit of advice to any drama major, high school theater kid ... write your own part. It is the only way I've gotten anywhere. It is much harder work, but sometimes you have to take ***destiny*** *into your own hands."*

IN THE FIRST SHOWS OF *MATT & BEN*, MINDY AND BRENDA WORE BRENDA'S BROTHERS' CLOTHES!

They wrote *Matt & Ben*, an hour-long play about the friendship between movie stars Ben Affleck and Matt Damon. Mindy played Ben Affleck and Brenda played Matt Damon. It won Best Play at the New York International Fringe Festival!

The Office

Matt & Ben was so successful, the show moved to an off-Broadway theater! Mindy and Brenda took the show to Los Angeles too. Once in Los Angeles, Mindy got a job that would change her life. She was hired on a new TV show called *The Office*. Mindy was only 24!

FACTS BEHIND THE FIGURE

Because of *Matt & Ben*, Mindy and Brenda got a deal writing a TV show about their lives! However, the show wasn't made.

MINDY WAS THE ONLY WOMAN AND ONLY PERSON OF COLOR ON THE WRITING STAFF OF *THE OFFICE* WHEN SHE STARTED ON THE SHOW.

Mindy has said that the first year of writing on *The Office* taught her how to write comedy. She also played the **role** of Kelly Kapoor on the show.

Best-Selling Author

The Office was a huge hit on TV! Mindy wrote and appeared on the show from 2005 to 2013. She became a producer on *The Office* too. As part of *The Office*, Mindy was **nominated** for six Emmy Awards!

In 2011, Mindy's first book came out. *Is Everyone Hanging Out Without Me?* is a book of essays about Mindy's early life, **career**, and stories from working in Hollywood. It made the *New York Times* Bestseller List!

MINDY MET HER BEST FRIEND, WRITER AND ACTOR B. J. NOVAK, WHILE WORKING ON *THE OFFICE*.

Mindy's Own Project

After eight years on *The Office*, Mindy starred in a show of her own: *The Mindy Project*. With this role, Mindy became the first Indian American woman to play a leading role on a TV comedy! But Mindy didn't just star in *The Mindy Project*. She also wrote and produced the show.

FACTS BEHIND THE FIGURE

Mindy was the voice Taffyta Muttonfudge in *Wreck-It Ralph* in 2012. She was also the voice of Disgust in *Inside Out* in 2015!

MINDY BECAME KNOWN FOR WEARING HIGH-FASHION OUTFITS IN HER ROLE AS MINDY LAHIRI.

Mindy played a doctor named Mindy Lahiri on *The Mindy Project*. The role was somewhat based on Mindy's mom. However, Mindy's mom died soon before the show first aired in 2012.

Woman at the Top

Mindy was unique as both a woman and an Indian American woman running a TV show. But she didn't want to only be those things: "I never want to be called the funniest Indian female comedian that exists. I feel like I can go head-to-head with the best white, male comedy writers that are out there."

In Her Own Words

"I realized that there was no one really who looked like me and I was representing a larger group of women and I have to be really careful about it because it's a huge responsibility."

IN 2015, MINDY PUT OUT HER SECOND BOOK, WHY NOT ME?

This confidence helped pull Mindy through six seasons of *The Mindy Project*. The show ended in November 2017, and Mindy had become a star.

Making Big Movies

In 2018, Mindy appeared in *A Wrinkle in Time*. She was excited to be part of the movie as a life-long lover of science-fiction. Mindy was also was glad to be part of increasing **representation** in the **genre**: "I finally feel welcomed with open arms to something that has ignored me completely."

FACTS BEHIND THE FIGURE

Mindy's daughter, Katherine—or Kit as Mindy calls her—was born in December 2017. Her son Spencer was born in September 2020.

THE CAST OF *A WRINKLE IN TIME* WAS DIVERSE, SOMETHING MINDY LIKED ABOUT BEING PART OF THE MOVIE.

Mindy also was part of *Ocean's 8* in 2018. Based on several movies led by mostly male actors, *Ocean's 8* had a mostly female cast!

Creating a Future

In 2019, *Late Night*, a movie Mindy wrote about being a woman in comedy, came out. She starred in it too! In 2020, the first season of *Never Have I Ever* dropped on Netflix. Mindy created the show, which is partly based on her childhood. A collection of her essays called *Nothing Like I Imagined (Except Sometimes)* was also released in 2020.

Mindy Kaling made her own path when no one cleared the way for her. Her fans look up to her and her co-stars respect her for the hard work that went into her success. What will Mindy do next?

Mindy's Timeline

1979: MINDY IS BORN ON JUNE 24.

2001: SHE GRADUATES FROM DARTMOUTH COLLEGE AND MOVES TO NEW YORK CITY.

2002: *MATT & BEN* WINS BEST PLAY AT THE NEW YORK INTERNATIONAL FRINGE FESTIVAL.

2005: MINDY BECOMES A WRITER AND ACTOR ON *THE OFFICE*.

2011: *IS EVERYONE HANGING OUT WITHOUT ME?* COMES OUT.

2012: MINDY BEGINS STARRING IN *THE MINDY PROJECT*.

2017: HER DAUGHTER KATHERINE IS BORN.

2018: MINDY APPEARS IN *A WRINKLE IN TIME* AND *OCEAN'S 8*.

2019: *LATE NIGHT* COMES OUT.

2020: *NEVER HAVE I EVER* COMES OUT. MINDY'S SON SPENCER IS BORN.

Glossary

architect A person who designs buildings.
career The job someone chooses to do for a long time.
destiny A force that decides what will happen.
diverse Differing from each other.
genre A type or style of movie.
immigrant One who comes to a country to settle there.
intern Someone, often a student, who works somewhere for a time in order to gain experience.
nominate To suggest someone for an honor.
producer Someone who organizes, supervises, and helps pay for a project.
representation The way a TV show, movie, book, or other media deals with and presents age, gender, or ethnicity.
role The part a person plays.
sketch A short, funny skit.

For More Information

Books

Amara, Phil, and Oliver Chin. *Awesome Asian Americans: 20 Stars Who Made America Amazing.* San Francisco, CA: Immedium, Inc., 2020.

Uhl, Xina M. *Women in Television.* Minneapolis, MN: Minnesota Core Library, an imprint of Abdo Publishing, 2019.

Websites

Mindy Kaling
theconcernsofmindykaling.com/
Keep up with Mindy on her website!

Pixar Animation Studios: Inside Out
www.pixar.com/feature-films/inside-out
Find out more about the making of *Inside Out.*

Publisher's note to educators and parents: Our editors have carefully reviewed these websites to ensure that they are suitable for students. Many websites change frequently, however, and we cannot guarantee that a site's future contents will continue to meet our high standards of quality and educational value. Be advised that students should be closely supervised whenever they access the internet.

Index